WHENEVER I FEEL

DEVENDRA K MISHRA

Copyright © Devendra K Mishra
All Rights Reserved.

This book has been published with all efforts taken to make the material error-free after the consent of the author. However, the author and the publisher do not assume and hereby disclaim any liability to any party for any loss, damage, or disruption caused by errors or omissions, whether such errors or omissions result from negligence, accident, or any other cause.

While every effort has been made to avoid any mistake or omission, this publication is being sold on the condition and understanding that neither the author nor the publishers or printers would be liable in any manner to any person by reason of any mistake or omission in this publication or for any action taken or omitted to be taken or advice rendered or accepted on the basis of this work. For any defect in printing or binding the publishers will be liable only to replace the defective copy by another copy of this work then available.

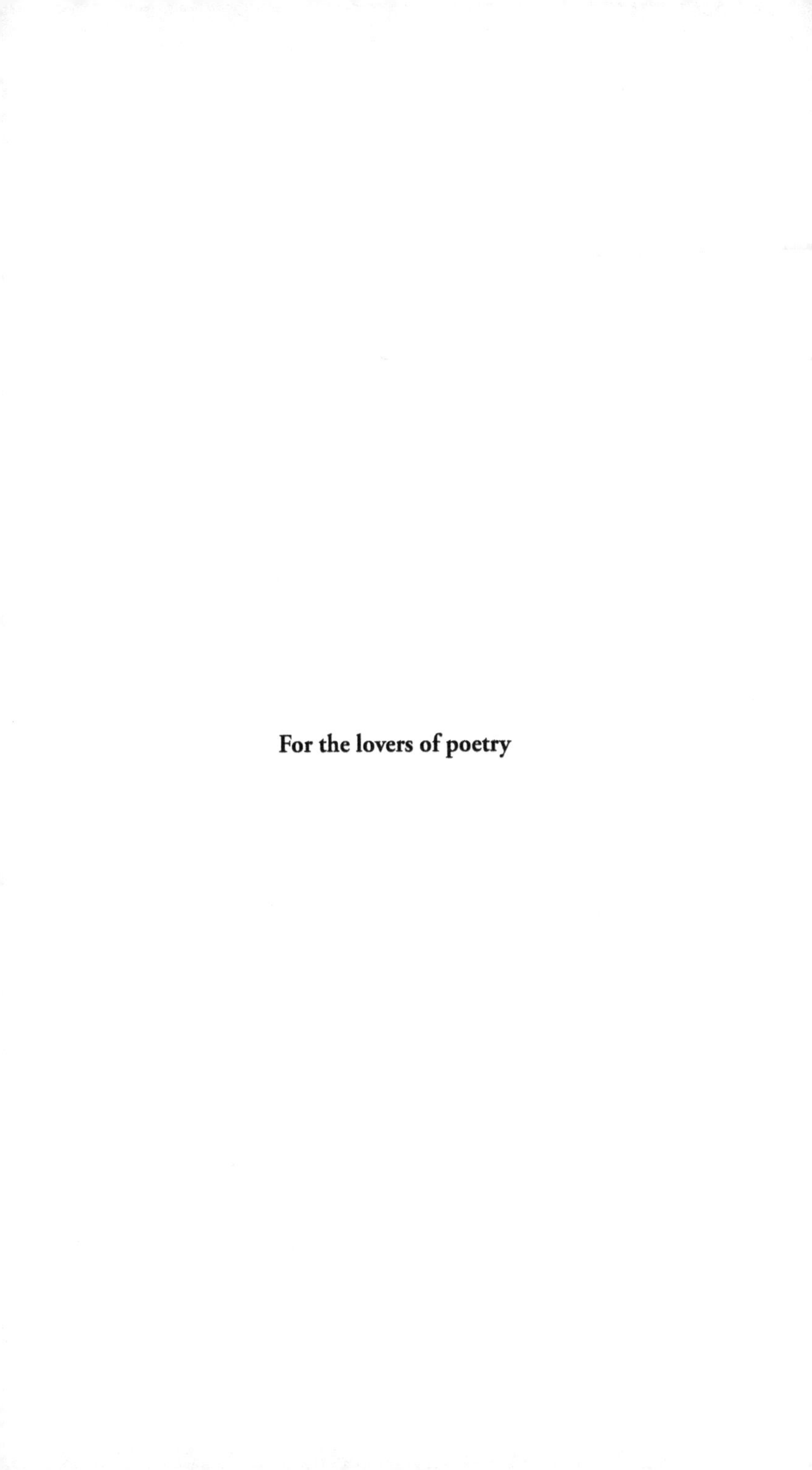

For the lovers of poetry

Contents

Contents

Acknowledgements

**Acknowledgments
I would like to
gratefully
acknowledge
the support
and encouragement
of all my acquaintances…**

Chapter1

Whenever I feel
sinking in the darkness
of my heart
I close my eyes
and walk down
memory lane
whenever I feel
drinking poison
of my bitterness
I leave myself
and stroll by the sea
thinking of you…

Chapter2

Terrible, dark
and fearful eyes
neither see nor weep
in their large sockets
they deadly glow
sun may shine
sea and sky may
display their blue
but these eyes
see nothing
only insanely scrutinize
the ashes of lives…

3. I Fear

I fear the sight
of the day
barking at me
I fear the bite
of season
infusing poison
into my senses
I fear the sudden knock
the door of solitude
receives
I fear the grass
that sprouts over
the tomb of hours
I enjoyed

Chapter4

Golden leaves
fall from the trees
gifting away their greenery
sun sets in
scattering its last ray
all over the sky
clouds die
pouring down
the last drop of its life…

Chapter5

Gentle breeze
dark bed of boundless water
hundreds of walking feet
gazers' delight
honeymooners' romance
vendors' livelihood
beggars' alms
a holy dip
for devotees
salvation for withered women
like a lightening
waves sparkle
tearing the blanket of water

Chapter6

Love me not so dearly, my dear
icy hands of death
are scratching my fate
seal me with
the sweetest goodbye kiss
like the final nail to a coffin
leave me alone to embrace
the inevitable
sunset of life
how SHE will dare
coming and stealing me
in your presence,
touch me not so tenderly, my dear
the eternal bond of life and death
is at stake

Chapter 7

Surprised
shocked and numbed
I found the doors shut
my father was an eternity
sitting in his rocking chair
all summer, rain, and winter
waiting for one and all
always ready to welcome
like doors of the home
I had a feeling
my father will stay forever
sitting in his favorite chair
going on healing us with his presence
I knocked at the door feverishly
it sounded, resounded, and echoed
but not responded
I was tired and drained
as if under the ruthless sun
looking for the shade
but no tree around
all of a sudden, I realized
my father is no more

Chapter8

Tell the sun to wait
moon to glow and stars to shine
she is coming
tell the winter to wait
spring to stay and cherish
she is coming
tell the tears to wait
smile to spread and deepen
she is coming

Chapter9

The name
I could never catch
but her smile was the contact
every Sunday,
I savored the smile
and rejected everything else,
neither a word
was exchanged
nor we ever felt for the same
one day,
she evaporated
like mist on a windowpane,
rain and sun
winter and fall
her smile is the only season I recall
the secret
of my placid life
will keep smiling even I depart…

Chapter10

The baby sun smiling
in the lap of a warm sky
gives me a thrill of joy
one day, my days
will come to an end
erasing all hope to amend
the pure delight
treasured in my soul
will delineate my eternal role
I will not be there
to behold the blue sky,
but no need to cry
You will feel me
in smiles and screams
embraced in sweet dreams…

Chapter11

A smell of mine will

dwell on you

even I

cease to be

sweet memories

will keep

your chilly night

warm and cozy

the starry night

will startle you

with sensuous

whispers

but the end of mine

can never lay

my love

to rest…

Chapter12

The blank pages
of my diary
waited for the ages
to get it filled
with live words
my childhood
got lost
in quest of
matured desires,
of adulthood,
and youthfulness,
unwittingly
vanished in
the vanity
of my folly
my gray-haired
look began
filling me
with unknown
fears
finally
the end of mine
scribbled the pages

DEVENDRA K MISHRA

with

live words…

Chapter13

Your tears
need no explanation
that I know
but still,
your tears
tear me into pieces,
don't waste
these precious pearls
for petty matters
may you need it
at the end of
my gambling with life…

Chapter14

We grumbled about our lives and cry
secluded and helpless
but our eyes are closed to…
the mirth of blue sky
the loving lore of gentle breeze
the joyful mood of dancing waves
the uneasiness of raining clouds
the pain of burning sun
the gloomy exit of the unwilling moon…

Chapter15

Take me away
I shouted
she was unmoved
take me away
I cried
she did not listen
take me away
I prayed
she smiled
take me away
I gave up
she touched me
with her cold fingers,
I lost all desires

Chapter 16

I run out of tears
but go on writing condolences
my spirits still soar higher
and haven't taken leave of senses
the ink of my pen dries out
and drowsiness takes me over
but my bleeding heart
tells me to move like a rover
life faces challenges
and plays with fire
endurance is the man
burns like a pyre
why do I allow fear
to eclipse my courage
and deface the soul
with my bloody image…

Chapter17

She came to me
made me cry
what a beauty
so great a joy
night so tender
calm and quiet
gave my imagination
an enchanting flight
one day she
sang a sad song
blaming our fate
for every wrong
with heavy hearts,
we bade goodbye
and once again,
it made me cry
letting her go,
was killing me
the life itself
negating me
time passes
memories remain
but my days are

never the same

Chapter18

I read stories
written in tears
I borrow sorrows
to kindle the light
I 'm a loser
I listen to the wailing
of weary wind
I 'm a loser
I feel a pull towards
unsung songs
I 'm a loser

19. Sun on the wet sky

Tender sun
on the wet sky
a toddler's smile
on his teary face

Chapter20

Her gaze
made me
a sun kissed
block of ice

Chapter21

My craving for you
is celestial
daydreaming of the moon
to a moonless night

Chapter22

Counted all its colours
and missed the rainbow
doing away with a flower
by removing its petals

Chapter23

Leave taking is a prelude
to revisiting
natural game of sunset
and rise

Chapter24

You are deep in my heart
either bloom or wither
spring and autumn
cherished by the nature

Chapter25

Your smile gives
meaning to my life
blissful rainbow
to a dull sky

Chapter26

Her warmth
stole me for ever
sun rays make
dewdrops disappear

Chapter27

Stillness endures pain
for survival
calm ocean welcomes
tempest's arrival

Request

Dear Readers,

I am eager to recieve your feedback and looking forward to seeing you with a new book.

Thanking you,

wheneverifeel531@gmail.com